BARREN RIVER

UNCLE JOHN PEMBERTON

ANDY HUGHES

HIGHLAND ROAD

JIM GREEN

HIGHLAND CHURCH

ROCKLAND

SALLY'S ROCK

GASPER RIVER

H. RIGSBY 1953

UNCLE BUD LONG

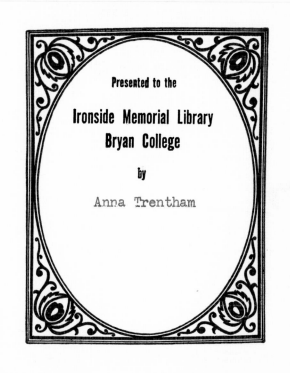

UNCLE BUD LONG

The Birth of a Kentucky Folk Legend

Kenneth W. Clarke

THE UNIVERSITY PRESS OF KENTUCKY

ISBN: 0–8131–1290–7

Library of Congress Catalog Card Number: 73–77252

Copyright © 1973 by The University Press of Kentucky

A statewide cooperative scholarly publishing agency
serving Berea College, Centre College of Kentucky,
Eastern Kentucky University, Georgetown College,
Kentucky Historical Society, Kentucky State University,
Morehead State University, Murray State University, Northern
Kentucky State College, Transylvania University,
University of Kentucky, University of Louisville, and
Western Kentucky University.

Editorial and Sales Offices: Lexington, Kentucky 40506

Contents

Acknowledgments

I wish to acknowledge the friendly interest of all the neighbors in the area served by Clark's Landing on the Barren River. I am grateful to Western Kentucky University for the sabbatical leave which gave me time for this and other interesting projects. I also wish to thank Harold Rigsby for preparing the illustrations.

INTRODUCTION

Where It Began

THIS is a study of the genesis of a legend, one important kind of literary origin. There are other headwaters of the great stream of our literary traditions, such as myth and ritual, or the simple oral recitation of events, real or imaginary. The spoken word everywhere preceded the written word. Folklore was the literature of all people before the invention of writing, and it continues to be antecedent to much creative writing even in our contemporary highly literate culture.

The legend-making activity considered here was quite fragile, so fragile that even this examination has altered it beyond recovery. The cycle of oral anecdotes was in its natural habitat, secluded, flourishing in its small way, but unknown beyond the vicinity of Clark's Landing. It was as natural as a patch of wild ginseng.

The analogy is an appropriate one. Ginseng is sought after more than any other herb gathered in the Kentucky forests. It is valued so far above yellowroot, bloodroot, fluxweed, and boneset that the people who gather wild herbs are commonly called "sang" hunters, sometimes more simply, "sangers." The plant grows slowly in certain locations having the proper conditions of soil and filtered sunlight. When the patch is dug up for the roots it is destroyed. One might ask why enterprising diggers refrain from planting ginseng in a garden to get a larger harvest. The answer is that domesticated ginseng is readily distinguished from the wild variety, and only the wild ginseng is prized.

So it is with legend. The authentic folk legend, like natural ginseng, is likely to be local and elusive, and is often passed by unrecognized. Once it is "dug up" or taken from its natural habitat, once it is even labeled "legend," it has ceased to be what it was and the folk quality of the narrative is diminished.

The authentic folk legend is fragmented, anecdotal. The usual domestication treatment is Procrustean—forcing it into some familiar literary guise to give it form (beginning, middle, end), continuity (missing elements supplied and transitions invented), and theme (moral or topical relevance according to the mood of the writer and the temper of the times). Having been thus domesticated to suit the writer's sense of literary propriety, the legend has assumed some form of written literature, has become more permanent than in its oral habitat, more subject to a continuing and expanding literary process, and more accessible to large numbers of people.

The genesis of American legends about Davy Crockett, Mike Fink, Daniel Boone, and Johnny Appleseed appears to follow a pattern. First was the telling and retelling; then came the attraction of familiar motifs to colorful character, expanding the oral cycle; then came the subliterature of newspaper columns, almanac lore, and promotional broadsides; then came the sweeping together of fact, fiction, and literary scraps for autobiographical or biographical treatment; and finally, with an abundance of precedent and materials to draw on, came the "creative" writer, the

4

sophisticated designer who worked his materials into a fabric suitable for his time and place.

Literature does not spring full blown, like Athene, from the author's brow, no matter how great his genius. His sources are many and often trace back to humble origins: "A feller said they was an old woman down the river that would go out and dig up a grave of a night. . . ." If we are to know the dimensions of literature and know them truly, we must continually renew our awareness of its sources and how they work. One of these sources, perhaps the primary source of all other sources, is the unsophisticated telling of a real or imagined event in the folk setting.

Examination of the legend-making or myth-making process is usually hampered by an overburden of literary invention. Robert Price, for instance, had to penetrate the literary facade to describe what had happened to John Chapman in his *Johnny Appleseed: Man and Myth*.[1] My own discussion of the Bud Long legend is unique in that no such overburden existed prior to this writing. The fragile legend was discovered quite unexpectedly, like the discovery of a patch of wild ginseng on a wooded hillside. As far as research can determine, not one scrap of writing about Uncle Bud Long existed until now, and the telling and retelling of certain anecdotes about him and his household has been confined to three generations of families who are or have been living in the vicinity of Clark's Landing, Warren County, Kentucky.

I had resided in the vicinity of Clark's Landing for more than a year before I became aware of anecdotes about Uncle Bud and his family. I believe this helps illustrate the fugitive nature of much American legendry. My sudden awakening came one summer day when a rather distinguished looking elderly man dropped in for a visit. He was Mr. Elvis Clark, passing through the neighborhood where he had spent his early youth. He remarked on his long absence, on how the countryside had changed, and on the similarity of our names. After we had concluded that we had no kinship and that he could hardly recognize old landmarks, he told an anecdote about Uncle Bud and his jennies. This reminded him of another, and yet another. I enjoyed a whole series of Uncle Bud yarns, expecting each one to be the last. Only when I was waving goodbye at the departing car did I realize in a kind of panic that I should have had the tape recorder on.

Once aware of the legendary Longs, I dropped their name here and there. Rarely was I disappointed in the spontaneous feedback I received. The Longs were, indeed, well remembered in the community, but the recollections were selective. The folk process of legend-making had been at work.

Although I tape-recorded a few interviews, I usually found the recorder to be a hindrance. Such a statement is near heresy among orthodox folklore fieldworkers, but my own experience with the tape recorder in this and other field investigations has not been uniformly satisfactory. Some informants appear to feel that the recorded interview is "official" in some legalistic way. They talk guardedly or not at all. In an informal visit, however, they chat freely about the Longs or any other neighborhood characters and events.

Another reason for avoiding a too-businesslike approach to the fieldwork was my feeling that the informants could easily become self-conscious or officious about the material they were giving me. In this instance it was important to retain a casual atmosphere, for I wanted to see the motifs in as nearly undisturbed and natural a setting as I could maintain. A few examples will illustrate.

I talked to Bester Cardwell on several occasions. The most satisfactory talk took place one evening when I drove by and saw him feeding stock in the barnyard. I drove in and leaned over the fence to talk to him. We had a good visit in the gathering twilight. I jotted down some notes when I got back into my car.

I talked to Earl Thomas on several occasions, once indoors with a tape recorder running, at other times outdoors as we went about such neighborly tasks as gathering turnip greens or finding

6

a good watermelon in his field. The recorded interview was the least productive of unguarded comments on the neighborhood and its occupants.

Avis Givens's little country store stands at the crossing of old Clark's Landing Road and Highway 231. Any time, winter or summer, a few local residents will be sitting around the stove on boxes and upended soft drink cartons. If I drop in for a loaf of bread I can join the random conversations. If I were to enter with a tape recorder all conversation would cease.

As my information accumulated I found that much of what I was learning was factual. It was about old roads, old families, old houses now gone, old stores, and old schools. It was the story of a way of life in an isolated folk community where the Long family had lived and worked for nearly twenty years. I realized, furthermore, that this information is essential for an understanding of the place and time of various legendary motifs about Uncle Bud. Accordingly, I have chosen to present a series of brief fictions, a day in the life of each of my principal characters. The fictions are, of course, based on facts. They represent a kind of averaging process designed to give continuity and avoid hyperbole or understatement. Since they are based on community research, they are more likely to convey an accurate impression than any number of documented texts and variants. A few verbatim texts are given in the discussion that follows by way of illustration.

Fortunately for the purposes of this study, historical records are of little value. The focus is on beliefs, attitudes, and entertainments rather than on documentary records. A few facts are helpful, however, in making an assessment of the fictions. The facts available are these:

Uncle Bud Long purchased his land in 1905. He was involved in various land transactions over the years. As late as 1915, he purchased a parcel of land for just over two dollars an acre. Apparently he was not a good speculator, for he sold forty-four and three-fourths acres for fifty dollars four years later.

Janey's "X" is marked once over the name "Martha Jane," once over the name "Marthy Jane." Her surname was not Long, and, correspondingly, Frankie's surname was not Long either. His first name, according to the records available, was Elija. He had two birthdays on the record, each one recorded twice.

It would appear, then, that Janey had been widowed, divorced, deserted, or separated from Frankie's father before the family moved to Kentucky. There is a suggestion that Frankie was born after they arrived. There is also a suggestion that Marthy Jane was Uncle Bud's stepdaughter.

Mrs. Long is the shadowy figure in folk memory. She is buried in an unmarked (now lost) grave in the small country churchyard. There are no sexton's records to establish the date or the precise location. Apparently she was shy or ailing or both. She is reported to have stayed inside the house when visitors were on the place. There seems to be no one living who was a member of the group that performed the primitive preparations for her burial.

The date of the Longs' departure from Clark's Landing is reasonably well established. A photograph of Janey was made by Veachel Cardwell, who took Josh Pemberton up to the shack and had him pose with Janey in front of the loaded wagon. Veachel had a reputation of being a prankster or tease, and he wanted to kid Josh about Janey. On the back of the original photograph is written "Bidding good-bye, Oct. 26, 1919."

The Setting of the Legend

THE western coalfields of Kentucky extend eastward along old ridges and escarpments largely covered by scrubby second-growth timber. They extend through Muhlenburg, Butler, and Edmonson counties until they taper off in the flatlands. Beyond the escarpments and in such unlikely looking places as front yards and barnlots one will see here and there a gas flare or an oil pump as a reminder that the coal formations are not far distant. Still further east, the pastoral beauty of the bluegrass region dominates the scene until the scarred earth of the mountainous eastern coalfields reminds the traveler of the wronged earth and the harvest of woes following the hasty earlier harvest of nature's bounties.

Warren County, Kentucky, is an in-between area. It contains a fair number of those not very productive oil pumps and a few stinking gas flares that still burn, but no sudden wealth emerged from either the oil or the rich coal seams, such as the one strip miners began to tear out of the earth in adjoining Edmonson County in 1970.

Part of Warren County is rich, moderately level farm land, yielding excellent crops of corn and tobacco. The portion that shades off toward the rugged foothills to the north and west is less good for crops, but suitable for pasture. The county is too far east to be part of the Jackson Purchase, too far west to be Bluegrass, too far south to share in the advantages of urban Louisville. In short, it is not a distinguished, spectacular, or notorious region, as is the poverty belt of the Appalachians, the scenic portion of the mountains, or the rich and romantic horse heaven of the Bluegrass.

Bowling Green, the county seat, is the site of Western Kentucky University, the county's chief cultural center, and for a very brief period it was the capital of the Confederate State of Kentucky, probably its chief claim to significance in history. Many of its citizens do their big-city shopping in Nashville, Tennessee, which is closer than Louisville, Kentucky's comparable metropolis.

The traveler who takes Highway 231 north from Bowling Green toward Owensboro will see a few good farms, but he will also be aware of the ridges of rocky, uncultivated land, signals of rougher terrain ahead. Not far from town he will see, if he looks in the right direction, a gas flare and an idle oil pump. A few miles farther north, he will dip down to an old iron bridge crossing a narrow, muddy stream, the Gasper River. Then he follows a steep, winding climb out of the river valley to a little crossroads community called Hadley. After a short distance on level road he will dip down another steep incline and abruptly up again. He will cross no bridge here but will drive over Clifty Creek and will probably be unaware of Clifty Hollow Road branching off to the right. Shortly after that valley crossing he will leave Warren County, enter Butler County, and arrive at Morgantown, population about 2,000, the county seat. There a coal bunker overlooks the Green River, an attractive, navigable tributary of the Ohio

River, and a reminder that this point, though related to the legend, is beyond the territory. The quickest approach to Bud Long Hill is to backtrack about fifteen miles and turn left onto Clifty Hollow Road.

The importance of Green River, though, would make the extra mileage worthwhile, for Green River, an avenue to the world at large via the Ohio, has a tributary, Barren River, which was also navigable, as long as its locks were maintained, as far as Bowling Green. Barren River also has a tributary, Gasper, which was that first muddy little stream crossing out of Bowling Green. Gasper River enters Barren River at Sally's Rock.

The fact that there was once regular traffic on Barren River is part of the reason for the once relatively populous nature of the area around Clark's Landing. Likewise, the disappearance of that river traffic is more than coincidentally related to empty schools and churches, to abandoned, brush-covered farms, and to little burial grounds now forgotten and lost in the woods.

To get to Clark's Landing, one travels from Bowling Green north to Clifty Hollow and turns right on a gravel road, which he follows for about three miles. Some old-time residents still call it Death Valley Road. A zig to the left at Rolling Springs Church and a zag to the right at Thomas's corner point one in a straight line to a white house and barnlot at the end of the road and on the bank of Barren River. Harold Clark (of an old Clark's Landing family) lives there and farms. Here is the end of the line for the lost motorist. He must turn around in front of Harold Clark's house and go back.

Harold Clark recalls that when he was a boy the steamer's whistle was a signal to him to find his nickel or dime, if he had one, then wait for the excitement of the smoke, noise, and churning sternwheel to subside as the gangplank was lowered. He was the first to board the packet, to race to the gustatory delights of the concession stand on board, and there squander his money on the sweets imported from the outer world—a welcome change for a boy's palate accustomed to little more in the way of treats than good Butler County sorghum molasses.

Back at the Clark home, travelers who had rested inside to await transportation were thanking their host and preparing for departure. Down at the barn, Negroes who had arrived on foot the night before and had slept in the hay were similarly occupied. A resident of Sugar Grove had already debarked and sought out the driver of the Sugar Grove freight wagon to be assured of transportation.

After the humming and singing Negro stevedores had carried the bundles, bales, and boxes across the gangplank, after the travelers had debarked and embarked, the noise of the engines resumed, with the bustle of winch and churning water. The *S.S. Evansville* headed toward the next stop, Sally's Rock, for mail delivery. Passengers would look for Sally Beck, the postmaster's daughter, who would stand on a natural chimney rock formation high above the river and hoist up the sack of mail with pulley and rope. Sally gave her name to the rock and a bit of picturesque activity to the river traffic.

Sally's rock was so distinctively slender and perpendicular that it was unstable. It collapsed into the river—fortunately late enough that Sally was not on it—and created a dredging problem for the river engineers.

The Sally's Rock (Rockland) post office is gone, as is most of the community it served. The quiet pastoral scene there, like the quiet pastoral scene at Clark's Landing or at Rolling Springs, seems to deny that Rolling Springs School once had over eighty pupils (first through eighth grade), most of whom walked to school and carried their lunches.

In those days, a team and wagon could deliver hand-hewn railroad ties to the big tie yard at Clark's Landing, then return empty past the grocery store, post office, and blacksmith shop at the Thomas corner, then along Clark's Landing Road over the ridge to the boundary of the old Cardwell place, and up Whiskey

Holler to the big spring just below the crest of the next ridge. There one would find Uncle Bud if he was not off trading or hauling ties, or Frankie, if he was not at school, or Janey, who was almost certain to be there.

From Uncle Bud's one could travel south, down past Clifty School to Vertrees' Store if he needed to trade, or he could go a short distance in the opposite direction over to the Hayes place if he had meal to grind, or he could continue in that direction to the Sugar Grove Road.

But one cannot take all those old routes today. Much of Clark's Landing Road exists only as descriptive detail on old property deeds: "beginning at a stake, a corner with Arthur B. Chapman and Herschel Brown; thence with Brown's line S. 47 E. 1749 feet to a stone in the edge of the old Sugar Grove Clark's Landing Road; thence with the edge of said road N. 53 E. 1412 feet to a planted stone on the northeast side of the Guy Clark's Landing Road; thence with the right-of-way of said road. . . ." But if one goes there to travel along that right-of-way, he finds an old fence line, and if he is lucky, a few traces of overgrown ruts in thickets of second-growth timber and sometimes impenetrable tangles of briars. There is no way of crossing the first ridge between Clark's Landing and Whiskey Holler without trespassing. Only a native familiar with a roundabout trail can get to the big spring without floundering through briar tangles and over fallen logs. And even a native will have trouble locating the little pile of weathered fireplace rocks—all that remain of Uncle Bud's cabin. Nature has swallowed up the evidence of a generation of residence, of the daily life of family work—hoeing corn, milking the cow, carrying water, feeding the chickens, and the heavy labor of felling, trimming, sawing, hewing, and hauling the massive oak crossties to the tie yard at Clark's Landing.

Paradoxically, civilized man's tenure on this piece of land is less evident to the present-day explorer than that of aboriginal man. The Indians who used the big everlasting spring, headwater of a tributary of Maxey Creek on Bud Long Hill, lived in natural shelters formed by erosion of the limestone ledge just below the crest of the ridge. A row of these shallow caves still shows some evidence of smoke from domestic fires, and on the outside ledges at convenient spots are deep bedrock mortars, called "hominy holes" by folks who live in the area and regard them as curiosities. The earth floors of the shelters are disturbed by generations of sifting, done by eager artifact hunters, who even to this day optimistically resift the siftings as though they have made the first discovery of an archeological site.

Indians were probably attracted to the place because it provided some natural shelter from the elements, a good view of the approach to the ridge, and a plentiful supply of good water. These same qualities would appeal to an independent mountain man accustomed to living close to nature. They evidently appealed to Bud Long when he brought his family to the ridge from somewhere in Tennessee at the turn of the century.

Although the cabin site seems quite isolated today, and although it was a little more isolated than some other homes in the area early in the century, Bud Long's place was not really difficult to reach. One could walk to the cabin from several different directions, the principal approach being a wagon road that ran along the boundary of the Elzie Clark place, then up past Hanging Rock and the upper boundary of the Veachel Cardwell place. These folks were neighbors—the kind who would borrow a cup of sugar or a thimble. Or, in more difficult times, they were the kind who would do the laying out, settin' up, and sometimes the burial on the home place.

All this is a reminder that a large portion of the Sugar Grove/Clifty/Rolling Springs/Guy/Hadley area was an isolated, inbred, self-sufficient folk community far into the twentieth century and that these traits are still clearly present to some degree, although the community is now in a state of rapid transition.

Because too much of the popular news media plays up the

easy cliche of isolation and cultural lag in the Appalachian region, there has been a tendency to ignore some of the equally isolated and often equally picturesque rural folk of other areas of Kentucky. This imbalance of exposure has been so great that most Americans know virtually nothing of Western Kentucky. Hardly any adult in the United States could now be unaware of strip mining problems in Eastern Kentucky, yet few adults other than some Kentuckians know that strip mining exists in Western Kentucky, let alone the desolation in large areas of the state quite remote from the eastern mountain area. Similarly, hillbillies (in the nonpejorative sense) are generally conceived to be crowded into the eastern mountains, yet one could hardly find better examples of hillbilly traits in the structures, speech, music, politics, and religion than those that turn up in portions of North Warren, Butler, Barren, and Muhlenberg counties.

For example, Uncle John Manning lived within loud hollering distance of Bud Long's shack. He died at the age of 73, during World War II, on the land where he was born. Uncle John didn't get far from home. He was taken to Bowling Green, about fifteen miles away, twice in his life—once to be signed up for social security and once to buy a suit of clothes. When he died in the 1940s, he was laid out at home by neighbors.

That degree of isolation resulted partly from lack of good roads. Eli Meador, for example, lived just at the foot of Whiskey Holler on Maxey Creek. He didn't have a road in from the east side, so when Earl Thomas carried a package to Mrs. Meador, he had to tie his horse at the edge of the Elzie Clark place and walk the last half mile.

Portions of the area waited until the 1940s for fairly reliable all-weather roads. Even with these developments, some of the older wagon roads were becoming impassable from lack of use and maintenance. When I wanted to talk to F. S. York, expert woodsman and blacksmith, I inquired the way to the century-old log house and was informed that I could not drive there, but that the now ruined road made the way unmistakable. I walked the mile or so to the top of the hill and was informed there by Mrs. York that her husband had gone to the store, by trail. The year was 1968.

Typical of many marginal farming areas of Western Kentucky, land tenure has been shifting away from the independent family unit in the Clark's Landing/Sugar Grove area.When Rolling Springs School had over eighty pupils, there were enough households within walking distance to keep the school well populated. Most of the students came from small family farms, like the Cardwell place. Some were children of tenants on larger farms, like the various tenant families on Squire John Hardy Thomas's large acreage. In any case, whether it was a land-holding family or a tenant family, the custom was to milk a cow, churn butter, gather eggs, can food from the garden, butcher a hog and a calf in season, grind sausage, dry fruit, and carry corn to the nearest mill for meal. Bartering with neighbors for goods and services took care of such extra needs as sorghum molasses, fodder, and horse shoeing. This left few needs to be supplied by purchase at the store: coal oil for lamps, needles, thread, fabric, coffee, salt, flour, and nails. It was a way of life. As Charlie Young remarked, "None of us had much, but they [the Longs] had less."

The old Horton house is a symbol of the period. It is a single pen log house, about sixteen by sixteen feet, with a small loft, a porch, and a large stone fireplace. It still stands, shaded by large trees, with its porch falling in, a kind of lonely landmark in the middle of a large field in which feeder cattle are grazing. The house just happens to be on one portion of a put-together acreage used by a modern, nonresident cattleman. But the old house, not as large in its total dimensions as some modern living rooms, served the needs of three generations of a family.

Though the old Horton house still stands, a larger home across the road has burned to the ground. Most of the old places have gone, usually by fire, sometimes by slow decay to such a point that the easiest disposal has been to push the structure into a gully with a bulldozer if the land is being cleared for grazing. Some of the old properties have been revived by absentee owners who have cleared away remnants of fences, barns, and houses, along with brush and trash trees to make pasture. Some still await this treatment. None is likely to be restored as an economic unit for the livelihood of a single family, for the north end of Warren County along the rocky escarpments is not generally suited to intensive, high-profit agriculture. If a growing family does live on one of the old farmsteads, one parent ordinarily works for wages to supplement the farm income and make it possible to have a reasonably comfortable way of life.

The lard press, sausage grinder, cider mill, grist mill, broadax, shake froe, forge, anvil, and walking plow turn up regularly at auctions, but they are not usually purchased for use. They are purchased, rather, for decorations and mementos, and are sometimes called "antiques," even by country people who have used them.

Charlie Young recalls that home burial persisted up to about mid-century. He would know this, for he learned the art of coffin-making from his father. He boasts that neither he nor his father ever took a penny for making one. "When you saw a fellow coming up the road with a stick from five to six feet long," he said, "and the stick was notched about a foot and a half from one end, you knew they had measured someone for a coffin." The length of the stick was for the length of the body; the notch measured the distance from elbow to elbow with the arms folded.

Mrs. Young added that it didn't cost more than about $1.75 to bury a person in those days. It took a few good yellow poplar boards for the plain box made in traditional coffin shape, a few yards of black broadcloth to cover the outside, a few yards of white broadcloth for lining, some tacks to fasten the broadcloth, and some screws for the lid. Neighbors cared for the body: women for a deceased woman, men for a man. It was the neighborhood women who went up to Bud Long's shack and took care of Mrs. Long's body when she died.

Many of the old traditions still run strong, for the older people stay and live out their lives on the land, whereas the young people follow what seems to be a national trend in their move to urban residence. Charlie Young and Earl Thomas, each in his eighth decade of life, are good storytellers. They are so good that they were persuaded to sit down in a color television studio and swap yarns. They complied with such natural ease that an old acquaintance who saw the show thought they had been filmed on Charlie's front porch.

Earl Thomas recalls with obvious nostalgia that he hauled the bricks for the chimneys of his home from Bowling Green with yoked oxen. The trip by modern automobile takes about twenty minutes. Earl's ponderous beasts took two days, making it necessary to camp by the river to keep track of the oxen on their overnight journey. Earl is thinking of breaking a team of heifers to yoke for old time's sake.

The transition from an isolated folk community to a modern rural area has taken place so rapidly that it has produced a variety of anachronisms. Tradition-rich Earl Thomas has a neighbor, Leon Chapman, who is a very energetic, successful, modern farmer. Leon exploits modern machinery and modern methods. He relies more on expert knowledge, advice, and printed literature available to career farmers than on formulistic beliefs and practices geared to the almanac and proverbial lore. Leon is one of the young, large-acreage, career farmers of a new generation and a new era in agriculture. Their number will increase as the older generation dies off, and the folklore of a region will be correspondingly impoverished.

Leon Chapman now owns the old Eli Meador place. Typical of the recent land consolidation trend, no one lives on the old place any more. The house is falling to ruin; the barn roof is slowly caving in and the orchard is dying out. But the portion of the farm that has good level fields is being cultivated at a rate greater than ever before, with heavy machinery, chemicals, and know-how that permits one man to do the work that several men did in times gone by. The uncultivated portion of the old place extends across Maxey Creek and up to the Bud Long spring. Leon and his boys go there sometimes to hunt, for game or for arrowheads. They never saw Bud or Janey or Frankie but they know about them. They never saw Bud Long's cabin but they can tell an inquirer where it stood. This means that Uncle Bud, Janey, and Frankie made enough of an impression to cause them to be talked about, not only by the old-timers still living who knew them directly, but also by the younger generation.

Uncle Bud loaded his family and household plunder on his short, high-wheeled wagon on October 26, 1919, and left Kentucky for good. But fifty-one years later, Fealon White, sitting by the coal stove in Givens's Grocery store, amused the Sugar Grove loafers present with a tale about Bud Long's chickens on the meal barrel.

HOW IT WAS

Uncle Bud's Day

BUD LONG awoke at dawn to the sound of Janey dropping the hot skillet lid on the hearth. The small room was only half-lit by the late summer sunlight slanting through the open cabin door. Bud stirred under the tattered, grimy quilt and noticed that Frankie was also in the process of waking up under the same cover. Up on a pole near the rafters a rooster flapped his wings and crowed.

Bud elbowed Frankie to hurry the waking process, put his feet on the ground, and pulled on his dirty, sweat-stiffened overalls. He didn't need to put on a shirt, for he always slept in his shirt tail. Without bothering to tie his brogans, he stumbled into the daylight and went straight to the thicket, a kind of open-air latrine off to the side of the cabin. From there he walked a few steps to the duck pond, a small body of water he had made by putting a dirt dam across the stream branch. Squatting at the edge of the muddy water, he washed his hands, wiped his wet fingers across his rheumy eyes, and with his fingers combed his orange-red, collar-length hair straight back, drying his hands in the process.

Having completed his daily toilet, Uncle Bud was ready for breakfast. Frankie, bringing a molasses bucket full of milk from the spring, joined him as he entered the cabin. Janey remarked on how the hens were laying as she took the egg-boiling can out of the fire. Bud swore at a clucking hen which had wandered into the cabin and was preparing to hop up onto the tumbled bed. The hen departed, still seeking an appropriate egg depository. Bud took the biscuit board from the top of the meal barrel where it had served as a table for Janey's meal preparation. He laid it across a mule-ear chair lying on its side on the ground. Here the biscuit board became an eating table. Bud sat on a low stool directly in front of the board. Frankie and Janey took similar seats, one on each side of the patriarch.

Uncle Bud dominated the meal. The skillet of bread and the bucket of milk were before him. He permitted Frankie and Janey to serve themselves from the side. Grasping the bucket by the brim, with his fingers extending down into the milk, Bud poured into cups held by Frankie and Janey, then raised the whole bucket to his beard-fringed mouth. The breakfast was simple, but not meager. Bud Long had a good cow. With plenty of milk, butter, buttermilk, and clabber, a family could keep hunger away if they had a little meal for bread and an occasional piece of meat.

Janey picked up the board, set the chair upright, placed the board back on the meal barrel, and put most of the remainder of the skillet of bread in a half-gallon molasses bucket for Frankie's school lunch. Bud reminded Frankie to bring in firewood before leaving for school, pushed the nanny goat away from the door, and walked toward the pole barn. He observed with approval the twin kids following the nanny. They would soon be ready for the meat box. At the barn, Bud picked up a short piece of rope and whistled for his jennies. The big mare was first to answer, but he ignored her and waited for three long-eared jennies to emerge from the brush back of the spring. He caught the pair he wanted, a work-worn gray and a younger brown. Harnessing was the work of a minute—collars, hames, and trace chains held up by bits of wire and string. When he hitched to his narrow, high-wheeled, flat-bed wagon, he handled singletrees and doubletree of his own manufacture, heavy, well seasoned hickory. Hickory could even supplant some of the hardware. The lapring of the near singletree was missing, but it had been effectively replaced by a hickory withe.

Bud threw his tie-hacking tools into the wagon: short cross-cut saw, chopping ax, maul, wedge, broadax, and branding hammer. Then he clucked to his jennies and headed up the ridge. Frankie was moving out of sight down the Elzie Clark fence row, capering and trotting like Miss Dee's riding horse. A fifteen-minute drive brought Bud to the end of the rough wagon trail cleared through the trees. He unhitched, shouldered his ax and saw, and led his team through the maze of trees and briar thickets to an area he was working out. Clean stumps and scattered brush piles attested to his industry. He tied his team and surveyed the standing timber. He had selected a cluster of about a dozen suitable trees the night before, and he had already felled three of them. Here was the beginning of a day's work.

Using a much-handled hickory stick, Bud measured the length of a railroad crosstie on the trunk of the first oak log and notched the spot with his ax. Moving on, he cut a second notch for a second tie, started a third, but stopped when he saw that natural taper had reduced the diameter of the log to a questionable dimension. Measuring with a notch cut into his stick, he verified the inadequate diameter, put away his measuring stick, and proceeded to saw off the first length.

Uncle Bud was a stocky, muscular man, about five-seven and 170 pounds. He threw his weight into a rapid, rhythmic stroke, observing that his saw was still sharp enough to draw shavings as long as his finger. By the time he had finished the first cut a patch of sweat the size of a lard bucket lid showed through the back of his ragged, work-stained shirt, and his inch-long beard glistened red gold in the sun.

He changed his pace by bringing up his team, hitching them to a chain choked around the end of the tie section, and skidding it out to where he had left his wagon. He skidded his log abreast of a pair of log sections laid parallel to each other about five feet apart. After he unhitched, he used a heavy hickory pole for a lever and a rock for a fulcrum. He lifted his tie-in-the-rough, one end at a time, and rolled it to where it was cradled in notches chopped into the supporting logs. He then chopped deep notches about a foot apart into the tie section. Using his hickory pry pole again, he rolled the section ninety degrees. Then he flattened the notched side of the log with his broadax, working from one end to the other, chopping off chips as much as a foot long with deft, powerful strokes. After that side was flattened, he pried his log once more and repeated the process for the other side. When he had finished his tie, Bud rolled it from its crude cradle, led his jennies back to the tree, and started a repetition of the whole operation.

By noon he had four finished crossties ready to load. He was strong enough to lift one end of a tie to the wagon by main force, but he was woods-wise enough to choose a less strenuous and more time-consuming method. Uncle Bud had his own way of doing things, mostly things he could do by himself. Frankie could help after school and on Saturdays, and Janey, strong as some men even if she was crippled, could bear a hand in a pinch, but tie hacking was a man's job. Bud could handle the whole operation with the aid of his nimble jennies.

He leaned a pair of eight-foot poles against the end of his wagon and pegged them together to make a loading chute. He blocked the wheels to keep the wagon from rolling, then hitched up and skidded the ties up to the bed, one by one. Perching on top of his load, he headed his team back toward the cabin. He didn't

26

drive. The jennies knew the routine and destination. He did, however, give them occasional verbal encouragement.

At the cabin, he ate a piece of cold bread and drank about a pint of buttermilk. Janey was off somewhere, and the goat was standing in the middle of the one-room living space, nursing its kids. Bud picked up an egg that had been laid in the middle of the bed and put it in the egg basket, which hung on a nail by the fireplace. Then he resumed his perch on top of the ties in the wagon, clucked to his jennies, and began the trip to Clark's Landing.

The jennies pulled hard to get up the hill, then braked hard to get down. The absence of brakes on the wagon caused it to roll forward. The absence of full harness on the jennies made it impossible for them to hold back by conventional means, so they had to hunker back and let the front end of the wagon ride up against their buttocks. Uncle Bud hunched over his rein strings, oblivious to the discomfort of the animals. His broad-brimmed, high-crowned hat was pulled down over his eyes, making it impossible for a bystander to tell whether he was dozing or merely impassive.

When his rig passed Virgil Simmons's blacksmith shop, Virgil looked up from his hoof trimming and waved his rasp in friendly greeting. A couple of observers remarked in undertones to each other on the sorry state of Bud Long's team and harness. When his rig passed the grocery store and post office, he responded to more greetings.

Squire John Hardy Thomas stepped out of the post office and hailed him. Uncle Bud pulled up. He liked the squire, the man who served the district as magistrate and seemed to feel that he was personally responsible for the welfare of everyone in the area. Squire Thomas inquired about the ugly sore, big and brown and wrinkled as a persimmon, on Bud's lip. Janey had treated it with poultices and a tincture of seven barks, but it persisted. Squire Thomas promised to have a doctor look at it. He would have a good doctor at his household in a week or two, and Bud should come.

Bud drove on. The distance between the post office and Clark's Landing was relatively short, and the monotony of the trip was much relieved by increased activity on the road. He hailed and was hailed in return. Two schoolboys hitched a ride on the back of his wagon. A fast trotting horse pulled a buggy past his plodding team and disappeared ahead of him.

Clark's Landing: No steamboat was in, but people were about. Uncle Bud observed that the tie yard was getting so full it was necessary to pile ties for shipment too far back from the landing. Soon a tie barge would arrive with a large crew of Negro stevedores. They would spend a day or two loading ties; then the empty yard would be a more convenient depository for him and all the other tie hackers in the area. When he got ready to unload, he went through a special procedure that he always saved for the last. He got out his branding hammer, went to the rear of the wagon, and struck the sawed end of each tie with one side of the hammer. The embossed initial on the hammer head left a deeply indented letter B on each tie. He reversed the hammer and struck each tie again. The indentation added an L to each tie: BL, his mark. No matter how many more came in, no matter how much the river might rise and float off property, Bud Long's ties were permanently marked for salvage or identification in case of mix-up. He sang his everlasting song as he unloaded:

> Daniel, Daniel, Dooshenberry, Dooshenberry,
> Daniel Dooshenberry, Dan . . . .

Uncle Bud had noticed that Frankie had picked up the endless song lately. It was a good tune, even if it didn't have many words.

When the empty wagon came abreast of Virgil Simmons's blacksmith shop again, Virgil waved Uncle Bud down. Bud was glad to stop and pass the time of day with a friendly fellow. The Justice boy and some other kid from school were tapping out a little tinkling music on Virgil's anvil. Virgil pretended to be much interested in the jennies, admiring them extravagantly and asking for a price. Bud, knowing that his diminutive team was the source of much amusement and derision responded with his usual banter: "Is that the truth, or are you just gassin'?" The blacksmith pretended concern for the near jenny's front hoof. It appeared to need trimming. Uncle Bud got down to look. As he stooped over the lifted hoof of the patient animal, the blacksmith backed up to the singletree and cut the hickory withe lapring with his sharp farrier's knife.

Having satisfied himself that there was nothing really wrong with his jenny's hoof, Bud remounted his wagon and started his team. Simmons and the boys watched eagerly, waiting for the cut withe to part. Nothing happened. The hickory was so dried out and set in its shape that it held on the level pull. The only way it would part would be under greater strain—uphill or with a load. Deprived of his fun and feeling suddenly responsible, Simmons called Uncle Bud back and began hammering out a new lapring for the dilapidated wagon gear. Uncle Bud smilingly assented in his peculiar, amiable way that no one could interpret satisfactorily. Was he simple? Was he shrewd, with the simple air a part of his shrewdness? Or was he just different—being from somewhere in Tennessee, somewhere different enough to cause him and Janey and Frankie to be set apart from the rest of the community?

Of a Sunday afternoon a whole crowd of people might take a walk up past Hanging Rock and loaf around his place. Kids would run in and out of the shack; young folks would kid Janey; and their elders would visit or trade with Uncle Bud. Even after school a pack of children might wander up there and hang around till suppertime—not because they liked the Longs, or respected them, or even felt sorry for them, but because the Longs were a plumb curiosity. The funny thing about all those people gawking and poking fun was that Bud didn't seem to resent it. He even seemed to kind of enjoy the attention.

Bud returned to his cabin in the late afternoon. Janey was

stirring up a pan of bread and Frankie was stirring the fire. Bud unhitched the jennies and shooed them off to the brush-covered hillside to make their meal of greenbriars. He decided to sharpen his ax before supper and proceeded to busy himself with his tools. While he worked, Janey called the cow, dumped a little feed on the ground inside the cabin door, and began milking. It was a convenient arrangement, the cow's head inside the cabin door, her body outside. Janey had only to hobble around the beast and milk it. Uncle Bud wouldn't have had it otherwise.

Supper was the same as breakfast except for the addition of a few shavings from the ham. By the time the board was cleared and put back on the meal barrel, dusk had settled into the hollow. Light to see by came from the embers in the open fireplace. Bud Long's cabin had no windows, and though the door was open practically all the time, the fire was always handy for illumination. Bud was first to bed. His simple preparation consisted of removing his shoes and overalls. Within five minutes he was snoring peacefully. When Frankie slipped in beside him, he hardly stirred. Janey busied herself beside the fire for a while, but she too retired early, taking the narrower board nailed to the wall at right angles to the rude bunk-bed occupied by her father and her son. The Long family shared their roof with the chickens, and they tended to keep similar hours.

Janey's Day

Janey awoke at the first call of the big rooster. He had gotten into the loft through the hole in the gable end of the cabin, and he was in a better position to notice first daylight than she was. When she sat up her straw tick made the same kind of rustling sound the rats made under the bed. Dad and Frankie were still asleep on the adjoining bunk.

Janey completed her dressing by slipping into a heavy denim skirt and putting on a pair of clumsy man-style brogans. She had worn her blouse to bed, and she wore nothing underneath, not even stockings. She hobbled immediately to the open fireplace, brushed back the ashes, and blew a cluster of embers to life. She reflected as she brought the fire to life that she hadn't used a match to start a fire for months—a year, maybe.

The cow had her head in at the doorway already, looking for feed and wanting to be milked. Janey pushed her aside as she hobbled out to the duckpond to get water. The dew lay heavy on the weeds and brush, but sunlight was filtering down through the trees, promising a pleasant day. Her peculiar rolling gait caused by her bent and shortened leg made carrying water in a pan difficult. This accounted for her habitual use of the duckpond rather than the spring above it for cooking water.

Back in the cabin, Janey got meal from the barrel and made a mental note that it would have to be replenished. She used the buttermilk she had set aside the night before, grease from the old coffee can, soda, and salt. She had her cornbread in the skillet and hot coals heaped on its lid in about two minutes. When water in the tin can she had set in the fire began to boil, she dropped six eggs in it to cook. While the eggs were cooking, she dropped some feed in front of the intruding cow and milked her. She would hold this milk for the cream to rise and use skimmed milk from the spring for breakfast. When she removed the hot lid from the skillet, it slipped and clanged on the hearth. Dad sat up, stirred Frankie, and got dressed.

When Frankie was ready to go out, Janey told him to bring fresh milk from the spring and more wood for the fire. Already it was quite warm in the cabin. Later on it would be plain hot.

With breakfast over, Frankie off to school, and Dad gone to the woods, Janey began her private day. She washed out the breakfast things, piled ashes back on the fire, and went outside. She had her basket things in the shade of a chestnut oak between the house and the barn. There she sat on an old chopping block with its top smoothed and rounded off by countless ax blows.

Janey had long, work-hardened fingers, muscular as a man's, but quick and supple. She wove the oak splints into a Tennessee basketweave with ease born of practice, and sang as she worked:

She rode up to Lord Thomas' door
And knocked and pulled the ring
And none was ready as Lord Thomas himself
To rise and let her in . . .

32

Uncle Bud Long posing with one of his jennies.
Photographer and date unknown.

Courtesy of Mr. Will Thomas

Uncle Bud Long sitting on a load of six hand-hewn crossties. Photographer and date unknown.

Courtesy of Mr. Harold Clark

She used the high mountain soprano when she sang song ballads like that, though her speaking voice was husky alto, the same voice she used for common songs like Daniel Dooshenberry. She reflected on Lord Thomas choosing the dark girl instead of the fair girl. Dad had once said it served the damn fool right. He should have stuck by the white girl anyhow. Maybe it just meant light and dark complexioned, though. Janey couldn't decide if she would pass for light or dark. She had green eyes, orange-red hair, and swarthy skin. But maybe if she got cleaned up good and didn't stay out in the sun so much, she would be fair as Lady Annet herself. But then Lady Annet didn't have a crooked leg, so it wouldn't be the same, anyway.

She couldn't decide whether she was attractive to a man or not. Some of the young fellows who came and hung around would get familiar enough, but maybe they were only like the jack when one of the jennies was in heat. He didn't seem to worry about how attractive they were. She had tried different things to see how the boys and men reacted. There was one time when she had a sudden impulse and dropped flat on her back and stuck her foot up for Hershel Hayes to see—said she had a thorn in her foot and would he take it out. He had a good look, certainly, but seemed more embarrassed than anything else. And the man with Hershel made a big joke of it. Then there were the smaller kids, always curious. She noticed how one of them hunkered down and looked real thoughtful on the opposite side of the cow when she was milking. She had just kept on milking and let him get a good eyefull. He would see plenty more than that before he grew up. Even Frankie had to have his curiosity satisfied, which was no difficult thing, seeing as how they all slept together and used the same brush thicket in place of an outhouse.

Mother had gotten after Dad about an outhouse and cutting windows into the cabin before she died, but he had put her off. Whenever Janey mentioned improvements like that he put her off, too, so there didn't seem to be any use. They might as well be up past the spring living in one of those Indian caves. The cave would be cleaner and wouldn't have as many rats and lice as the cabin had. It wouldn't be much colder in winter, either.

She finished the basket and set it aside. One of the Clark girls had spoken for a basket. Some evening soon Janey would walk down to their place and deliver it. That would mean twenty-five cents to do as she pleased with.

As she started for the cabin, she caught a sudden movement in the corner of her eye. She stopped and looked down at the thick, shiny coils of a timber rattlesnake. As she looked, its tail, ridged like a small ear of corn, began to vibrate, sending out a bone-chilling warning. Janey detoured around the buzzing snake, got a hoe, and returned to kill it—one more bellboy dead. The ridge was full of them in summer, which would be enough to keep ordinary folks from living there.

She knew her dad was no ordinary man. He drove jennies because he didn't have to feed them. He wore his old rags till they fell off even though he had a wad of bills as big as his fist down in one of those tattered pockets. It was like him to choose a place to live way up on a hillside out of sight of anybody and expect his family to live the way he did, like a pack of groundhogs. He said it wasn't right or natural to wash with soap. Said natural skin would keep off chiggers and ticks. He was probably right about that. She had scrubbed herself clean and sweet-smelling once with a bar of store-bought soap Nellie Cardwell had given her. The chiggers like to ate her up until she got back to natural again.

Nellie Cardwell was a small, slender woman like Janey. Nellie gave Janey some nice clothes she was through with, but Dad wouldn't let her wear them. He said the Longs were not rich, but they weren't beggars, either. If he could wear denim overalls, she could wear denim skirts. Up there with the snakes and briars those fancy clothes would give out too soon, anyhow.

Janey got a grass sack at the cabin, went to the corncrib, and began shelling out a turn of corn for the mill. The big blacksnake that lived under the crib watched her, tame as a cat. It stayed there all the time and ate mice. Dad said a good blacksnake was better than any dozen cats for keeping mice down. He wouldn't ever kill one, even if it got in the cabin. Janey sang about Barberry Ellen and her troubles with Sweet William. It seemed as though people in the olden times had troubles that were even worse than the ones suffered by the people that came after.

When she had a turn of corn ready, she tied the sack and whistled for the jenny she had seen poking its head around the corner of the barn. It came for a handful of corn. Janey caught it, put on a bridle, mostly string and wire, and cinched on a tattered, rat-gnawed side saddle that had belonged to her mother. It had been a good saddle once, with red and orange figured carpeting on the seat. It must have been something left over from Mother's people. She threw the sack of corn over the jenny's back behind the saddle, mounted, and headed for the Hayes place.

Hershel Hayes had the nearest gristmill. There was a bigger mill up by Clifty School and another at Sugar Grove, but unless Dad was going to Vertrees's store or to Sugar Grove to trade it was more handy to carry the corn to Hershel's mill. Dad always told her to watch the milling and make sure the miller didn't heap up his toll dish, said there wasn't ever a miller to be trusted. Lots of people must have felt that way. She knew the words to "The Old Steam Mill," a song about a miller who tried out all his sons on tolling to see which one would heir the mill. The one that would cheat the most got it.

She timed her arrival to catch Hershel in for dinner. He could start the engine anytime there was meal to grind, but unless it was dinnertime or suppertime, he was likely to be out working somewhere. She didn't have to worry about Dad's dinner. If noon came and he was busy in the woods, he didn't eat, and if he happened to come by the shack at noon, he would generally fix himself something. Mrs. Hayes and her granddaughter were clearing the table when Janey got there. Hershel was still there, so he ground the

35

corn. She didn't bother to watch. She knew the Hayes family wasn't poor enough to steal corn or meal. In fact, once when she had loaded the meal on her jenny to return home, she had overheard Mrs. Hayes telling one of the children to throw the toll to the chickens. People as well off as that wouldn't have to cheat.

On her way home, Janey got thoughtful about the bustle at the Hayes place. Mrs. Hayes was clean and smiling, so different from how Mother had been. Mother got awful tired on that long wagon trip from Tennessee. She never had settled down or caught up in the cabin they moved to. She had wanted windows and a floor. Dad had put her off on the windows, but he had brought up some rough tie lumber and laid out a part of a floor in front of the fire. Mother had acted ashamed of the place when people came. She would stay inside and not even peek out if a visitor happened to be on the place, and she would hide out in the woods if a crowd came of a Sunday. The move and the hard life were too much for her. She just pined away, died in bed from whatever ailed her. Dad tried to be nice to the women who came up and laid her out, but when he rummaged around under the bed Mother was laid out on to get the ham, the ladies all looked thoughtful and none of them would eat anything. Mother would have wanted to be buried back in Tennessee, but the best Dad could do was to carry her down to the cemetery at Rolling Springs and put her in the ground in a homemade coffin.

When Janey got home she found Bester Cardwell playing with the dead snake. He wanted the rattles. Janey took her Barlow out of the deep pocket in her skirt and cut them off for him. Bester was an independent acting little boy a year short of school age. Since Frankie was in school it got lonesome during the day, and it was nice to have a boy playing around the cabin again. Sometimes she asked him to stay and eat, but he always took that to be a sign that it was suppertime at home.

She brought the embers in the fireplace back to life, piled on enough wood to make broiling coals, and went to the spring for the rabbit. Frankie, always handy with traps and snares, could be counted on to produce a rabbit or a possum or a quail every day or two. He had brought in a rabbit the day before. Janey had dressed it and put it in a lard bucket at the spring. Back at the fire she tied the whole rabbit by the hind legs to a string attached to a nail over the arch rock. After it got good and hot, she would give it a turn occasionally to keep it turning in front of the fire.

Frankie came in from school and put the syrup bucket he used for lunch down by the meal barrel. Janey sent him for wood. Bester looked in, noticed the supper preparations, and decided to go home. Janey could hear the wagon coming up to the barn, so she got some of the new meal and started bread. Frankie came in with wood and told her how Combs Hicks had been badgering him about who his father was. Frankie needed to know some things, but Janey wasn't ready yet to talk to him about family.

Dad came in from the barn, sniffed approvingly at the briskly broiling rabbit, and proceeded to tell Janey and Frankie how he had gotten a new lapring that hadn't cost him a cent. Dad was like that—enthusiastic about anything that would save him a nickel or a dime. But even if Janey saved him all kinds of money making clothes, he wouldn't spend a few cents for a thimble.

Darkness fell fast after supper. Janey cleared away the few dishes, replenished the fire, and watched her father pull off overalls and shoes, his only preparation for rolling onto the rustling straw tick which covered the rough boards of the bunk nailed to the log wall. Frankie waited till Bud was asleep before he turned in.

Janey waited to let the fire die down so she could cover it. She watched the two men of her life sleeping under the same cover on the larger bunk. Her bunk was nailed to the other wall, making a right angle from the foot of the bigger bed. Sleeping together like this, yes, all three in the same bunk if the weather got bitter, made her wonder whether her relationship with her father was more like that of a wife than that of a daughter. Some other people wondered too, she knew. She told everybody that she and Frankie bore another name, but it didn't seem to make any difference. People still called her Janey Long and they called her son Frankie Long, and newcomers were likely to assume that Uncle Bud had a young wife and a child of his old age. She slipped out of her skirt. It was another day like hundreds, even thousands, of other days end to end, without any change except the weather and the seasons.

Frankie's Day

FRANKIE trotted down the Elzie Clark fencerow, slipped
through a gap where a paling was broken, and cut across the corn-
field to the Cardwell barn. He was early, so he didn't show himself
at the house. He set his lunch bucket on the ground and perched on
the end of Mr. Veachel's big feed trough. There was no sound except occasional stamping and snorting from the mules in the barn.

Frankie looked down the length of the trough, made by hol-
lowing out a big cedar log. If he had it in the river he could travel
anywhere he pleased, away past Bowling Green and clear out of
this cussed Kentucky country. He didn't know any other country,
but Grandpa always said this cussed country and talked about back
home in Tennessee.

He sat and wondered about Tennessee until Maude came out
of the house with her lunch and books. He picked up his bucket
and joined her. They walked down the hill and followed the wagon road to the Jasper Clark house. Alma joined them, and they

continued toward school, finding more company as they went.

Maude teased Frankie about his singing; then the other kids joined in, and kept asking him to sing a song. He knew they were making fun, but he enjoyed the attention anyway. Finally he gave in and sang the song he had made up:

> *Come all you good people, serve you wrong.*
> *You asked me to sing you a song.*
> *I asked you what that I must sing.*
> *You told me to sing anything.*

Frankie sang in a loud, harsh voice, but his tune was true. The kids were satisfied for right then, but later on someone would be sure to ask for Daniel Dooshenberry.

The big boys like Earl Thomas and Willis Justice didn't bother him much. They had plenty to do keeping up with the pranks they played on each other. The older Thomas boys were especially good at making trouble or doing things nobody else would do. They swam like eels in the river, doing dangerous things around the paddlewheels of the steamers that stopped at Clark's Landing. Frankie couldn't even swim. He had never had a chance to learn, since Maxey Creek didn't have water enough for swimming, and he never played away from home.

At school some of the boys were playing ball while they waited for the bell to ring. Frankie watched. When Mr. Will got ready to ring the bell, Frankie raced inside to be the first one to take his seat. He tried to be first in when the bell rang and first in from recess. He tried to read louder than anyone else, and he tried to think of good questions to ask Mr. Will, but no matter how he tried, he couldn't seem to get ahead of the girls who could read so fast or the boys who could cipher in their heads. The big boys, some bigger and older than Mr. Will, treated Frankie like a little kid, and the big girls, some bigger than Ma, acted like they wanted to take care of him.

40

Frankie didn't enjoy the morning because all he had to do was work multiplying problems and memorize spelling. He didn't get to recite once. He was glad when dinnertime came. He took his lunch bucket over to the trees by the gully on the lower side of the school. He always tried to eat alone because the other kids tried to see what he had, and he never had very much. Nobody followed him. He opened his molasses bucket and wolfed down the piece of cold cornbread, wishing he had milk to go with it.

Some of the younger boys began playing marbles in the dust beside the one-room school building. One boy drew a laggin line with his toe. Another drew a fatty hole with a stick. Frankie moved closer to watch. He didn't have any marbles, but if he did, he was sure he could beat any of them. Earl Thomas nudged him and held out a jelly sandwich. Earl said he had more than he could eat. Frankie thanked him and promptly gobbled up the sandwich. Earl was older than Frankie, but he was a younger son of Squire John Hardy Thomas, who had six boys, all of whom were regarded as holy terrors in the neighborhood. Even so, Earl was generous with his lunches. He almost always had more than he could eat.

Mr. Will rang the bell just in time to prevent a fight between Andy Manning and another marble-playing boy. There was a fight almost every day, but Frankie didn't get involved. He wasn't involved in ball games or marbles, so he didn't have many arguments. Sometimes he would join the chase in fox and dog, but that didn't take much talent.

Grandpa drove by with a load of ties during afternoon recess. Some of the big boys ran out in the road and grabbed the wheels of the wagon, bringing it to a stop. The jennies had four ties to pull, about as much as they could handle. Five or six strong boys hauling back on the wheels could prevent them from moving. Grandpa just sat on his load and smiled and sassed back at the teasing boys. He didn't offer to cuss them or whip them. Finally, when they had shown off enough, they let the wagon go. Frankie stayed in the shadow of the schoolhouse all the while, hoping Grandpa wouldn't see him, half wishing the boys wouldn't do that and half wishing he could join them in their boisterous fun.

When school let out, Frankie ran out ahead of the crowd of children. He wanted to get home in time to go up on the ridge to check his traps. Besides, Grandpa had scolded him for loafing around with boys who went to the landing after school. Said there was nothing but mean acting and mean talking amongst most of these modern kids. A boy should learn to mind his manners and make a living. That meant learning how to chop with an ax and hoe corn. Frankie did give in to the temptation to stop for a while and watch the big steam engine at the sawmill on the Horton place. The engine poured out a cloud of smoke and pulled a tremendously long belt that ran machinery he didn't understand. The noise of the headsaw almost hurt his ears. He couldn't help comparing the big, well-harnessed teams with Grandpa's jennies. The big log outfits made the little road wagon and its team of jennies look mighty puny.

When he got home, Ma told him to bring wood. He could hardly turn around without being told to bring wood for the fireplace that ate up armloads day after day. He got the wood in, took his coon-killer club, and went up on the ridge to see about his traps. He had two steel traps that were best of all, five box traps that were pretty good, and any number of wire snares that hardly ever caught anything.

One steel trap was sprung, with nothing in it. The other was sprung too, but it held the toe of a raccoon. The animal had bit its own toe off after it got caught. One box trap held a possum, which Frankie clubbed and carried by its tail. None of the snares had caught anything.

He carried the possum home. Ma would fix it in the coals with sweet potatoes for a special meal. He had a feeling of success, enough success to consider this day as good as any other, better than most.

WHAT IT MEANS

The Narratives as Folk Literature

THIS small cycle of Bud Long tales was recorded when the tales were not yet corrupted by literary influence of self-conscious rendition. Thus they are useful for inquiry into the process of folk selection, retention, and re-creation of entertaining narrative. We are fortunate to have here a relatively small body of material that has not had enough distribution in either time or space to attract journalistic or historical treatment and thus begin a trend of magnification or distortion.

By way of comparison, one might examine William Hugh Jansen's "Abraham Oregon Smith: Pioneer, Folk Hero, and Tale-Teller."[1] In this excellent study, Jansen was able to develop the point that historical information was likely to be at odds with what had been preserved in legend (p. 340), and that the survival of the tale-teller's reputation had been partly dependent on successors in that art (p. 342). Jansen could not, however, get at the germination of the Oregon Smith cycle because the Indiana-

Illinois folk hero, though less widely known than Johnny Appleseed, had nevertheless become a part of the documentary and journalistic record. Jansen, then, like Price in studying Johnny Appleseed[2] or Dorson in studying Davy Crockett,[3] necessarily expended much effort on the problem of separating verifiable historical data from unverifiable legendary material.

No effort will be made here to evaluate the historical accuracy of the narratives relating to Bud Long. The focus is rather on the significance of this microcosm of folk narrative in the world of literature and literary criticism.

Cursory examination of the *Motif Index of Folk Literature*[4] reveals that certain categories of narrative motifs have had worldwide popularity, both in the oral traditions of the folk and in subsequent literary adaptation. Since formal written literature had its origins in the recording of already established folklore, and since the subsequent development of written literature has continued to be nourished by folk traditions, in spite of the separate conventions of art literature, it is profitable to examine the streams at their sources.

Dominant Motifs in the Bud Long Cycle

TRICKSTER

The perennial popularity of the trickster, whether he be a master thief, a cunning fox, a secret agent, or an outlaw in Sherwood Forest, has been a subject much analyzed. The tendency of the folk to develop cycles of tales about the trickster supremacy of such an unlikely creature as a rabbit, for instance, has been cited as a kind of identification—the weak or helpless common people in the role of rabbit overcoming tax collectors, knights, or kings in the role of bear or wolf. Complications of trickster motifs sometimes involve dramatic reversal, the trickster tricked; or the trickster tricked but regaining supremacy by additional trickery.

46

1. One day when Uncle Bud was driving his jennies back from Clark's Landing, Virgil Simmons, the blacksmith, told the boys loafing in his shop that he would have some fun with the old tie hacker. When Uncle Bud came abreast of the shop, Virgil stepped out to visit. He pretended to admire the team, praising the jennies extravagantly, and with a ruse, distracted Uncle Bud long enough to cut a hickory withe that had been substituted for a lapring. He expected it to pull apart when Uncle Bud started to drive off. Then everybody could laugh at the old, patched-up gear when it came apart. But the withe was so hardened with age that it held anyway, and the jennies started on up the road with the wagon as though nothing was wrong. Then Virgil got worried because the ring could pull apart on a hill with a load and maybe hurt somebody, so he called Uncle Bud back and forged him a new ring.

This episode has been retained because it has the satisfying element of a trickster at work on a practical joke. The fact that the joke failed is satisfying also, for the harmless intended victim comes off well in the end.

2. Veachel Cardwell used to hire Uncle Bud to work by the day sometimes. In those days a hired hand always took his dinner with the family he worked for. Nellie Cardwell was an exceptionally good cook, and on this particular day, she had made a big peach cobbler. When they had dinner, Veachel took a little piece, Nellie took a little piece, and Bester, if he was there, took a little piece, and that left at least three-fourths of that big cobbler not eaten. Veachel was curious to see just how much Uncle Bud would eat, for he knew Bud didn't have any fancy grub at home. So Veachel kind of

47

insisted that Uncle Bud help himself and finish off the big cobbler. He did. He ate every bit of it. Then he got such a bellyache in the afternoon that he couldn't work. So Veachel's joking kind of backfired on him.

This narrative is similar in some ways to the one about "punkin bread" below (no. 5). It is different, however, in that it contains the trickster element of the practical joke that backfires.

3. Uncle Bud used to take eggs to the store to trade, you know. He had a little old home-made basket, and he would take a basket of eggs to the store. Well, lots of times there were some mischief-making boys hanging around the store, and they would slip around and drop some new nails into Uncle Bud's basket. Then Uncle Bud would find the nails and act real puzzled. He would go over to the storekeeper and say, "Are these my nails in this basket, or did those pesky boys put them in there?" And the storekeeper would look and say, "Nope, they aren't mine. Must be you had some nails in there and didn't notice." So Uncle Bud would keep the nails.

This narrative contains a trickster prank, such a gentle one that it adds a pleasant touch of charity to the characters of the boys and the storekeeper. It also adds another insight into Uncle Bud's char-acter—his shrewd acquisitiveness leading him to exploit his image in the community.

NUMSKULL

One suggested explanation of the great popularity of numskull motifs is that the in-group using the narratives can momentarily enjoy the feeling of superiority that derives from laughing at the

Josh Pemberton poses with Janey beside the loaded wagon on the day of the departure. The photograph was taken by Veachel Cardwell.

Courtesy of Mrs. A. B. Chapman

stupidity of others. We can observe that ethnic, regional, occupational, and other forms of bias are commonly present in numskull narratives. Also, there is some interplay of trickster and numskull motifs. The trickster who persuades his victim to put his hands or paws in the wedged-open cleft of a log is being a trickster when he knocks the wedge out, but the victim is also a numskull to be so easily duped.

> 4. One day two boys who were haying on the Cardwell place got hot and thirsty and decided to walk up to Bud Long's spring to get a drink of cold water. When they got there Uncle Bud invited them inside. Janey was cooking at the fireplace. When she turned around, the boys saw that her face was all streaked with something black. One of the boys asked her what she had on her face. "Sut 'n taller," she replied. He asked her why she had smeared her face with soot and tallow, and she replied that her saddle had turned and she had been thrown from a jenny into the briars and that her face was badly scratched. Uncle Bud put in that she wouldn't have had that trouble if she had taken the trouble to cinch her saddle up tight. She said she had taken it up as far as it would go, and that in order to make it any tighter she would have had to go round to the other side.

This narrative has persisted because it contains a satisfying numskull motif. The Long household never integrated into the social life of the community. As relative outsiders they were suitable subjects for ridicule. The point of the tale is that one usually adjusts the saddle girth as much as necessary, even if it requires that one go to "the other side" to take up the slack there. The narrative reveals that Janey knew this but was either too lazy or too short-sighted to take the trouble to make the necessary adjustment. An additional detail is the "Sut 'n taller" quotation, delivered with an emphasis suggesting that the informant considered such a primitive home remedy to be additional evidence of numskull backwardness.

> 5. Uncle Bud came down to a big logrolling at the Cardwell place. Everybody in the neighborhood came, and the women all brought food. It was kind of like a picnic. When it came time to eat, Uncle Bud was eating enough for any two men. One of the women had brought a nice yellow layer cake. Uncle Bud spied that cake, and he just slipped his knife between the layers and lifted the whole top layer off onto his plate. One of the women saw that and asked him if he wouldn't like some lightbread. Uncle Bud said, "No, Ma'am, this here punkin bread is good enough for me."

The familiar motif of the uncouth frontiersman has been attributed to many characters in many situations. The fact that it could (and probably did) really happen does not simplify the explanation of the popularity of such a narrative, however. The unique spirit of American humor derives in part from the willingness of Americans—writers, politicians, and actors—to capitalize on the rough and ready aspects of the American experience rather than to apologize for them. Here we see Bud Long joining such distinguished company as the fictional Jonathan in earliest American drama and Davy Crockett in later American history.

PEOPLE & ANIMALS

The popularity of some animal motifs may derive from another kind of identification—man's desire to fly, dig, see, smell, run, jump, or perform other feats as well as certain animals do. In some older forms of folk narrative the wish is fulfilled in fantasy by magic transformation. In other tales a faithful animal with extraordinary understanding may function as surrogate for its owner on a slightly more realistic level. Johnny Appleseed was able to communicate with wild animals. David of Sassoun's horse could warn his master of danger, as could the Lone Ranger's Silver.

> 6. Uncle Bud had hardly any harness, and he always worked these little jennies. He would have them hitched up in a team of two or four or even six. Generally he had about as many ties on his little old road wagon as he had jennies pulling—one tie for each jenny. Well, he could do marvelous things with them. He could come over that steep hill with a load of ties and no reins or bridles on the team. He didn't guide them, just talked to them. He could talk his team along as well as most people could drive with reins.

This narrative has survived because it contains the satisfactory element of a marvel—a strange (or eccentric) man who chose to use diminutive jennies instead of the usual mules or horses, and further, who could work them in a mysterious, unconventional way. Judging from numerous references to these animals, people were mystified, as to both why and how Bud Long worked them.

> 7. The chickens at the Longs' used to roost over the porch. It reminds me of the story my grandmother and grandfather used to tell about some old gal. Every night she used to say, "Did you turn the chickens?" The chickens were in the habit of roosting on the meal barrel. They had to turn the chickens so the heads would be pointed in toward the barrel instead of out.

The chicken-turning motif belongs to general folklore, but some version of it almost invariably turns up in a discussion of the Long household. The text quoted here seems to illustrate the transfer from general to specific in progress. Observe that this informant merely mentions chickens roosting on the porch (a puzzling observation in that no other description includes a porch), then states that he is reminded of a report of *another* person that his grandparents spoke of, a person who turned the chickens on the meal barrel. Legend-making thrives on such borrowed motifs.

TREASURE

Common currency in legend and literature is the motif of lost or hidden wealth. Buried pirate treasure, the miser's hoard, the lost silver or gold mine, and old greenbacks stuffed in the wall represent a continuation of the traditional motifs seen in the *Arabian Nights* and similar early literary monuments that stand close to their folklore sources. The ubiquity of such motifs appears to derive from wishful thinking projected into fiction, whether the projection be a folktale or a novel.

> 8. When Mrs. Long died, the neighbor women went up to the shack to do what they could. When it came time to dress the body, Uncle Bud opened a trunk, and it had all kinds of very fine dresses and other things to choose from in it. Here they had all these expensive things in a trunk, but they were always dressed in rags.

> 9. When his wife passed away, the neighbors went in to dress her. They said they found clothes that were put away in trunks or boxes that had been some of the finest clothes that you could imagine, silks and such. She must have come from quite a family, must have been well-to-do at one time. And whether it was true or not—I wasn't there, and I don't think my grandmother went there—but they said that there was dogs

on the bed, and they had to beat these dogs off to wash
her and dress her.

10. Uncle Bud always paid cash and never ran up a
bill at the store. He did some trading all the time, and
once at an auction he wanted a fine mare that was for
sale. He bid her up to ninety dollars. The auctioneer
was afraid at first to knock the sale down to this old fellow in rags and tatters, but when he finally did, Uncle
Bud dug down in those rags and pulled out a big roll of
bills, peeled off ninety dollars, and seemed to have
plenty left over.

These narratives have survived because they contain the satisfying
element of mysterious wealth in an unlikely setting. As one informant remarked, "People thought they might have more than
they showed."

Versions of Mrs. Long's "laying out" contain a range of
variation in detail, but allusion to fine clothing is one of the best
preserved and most circulated details in the community.

FUGITIVES

Especially if the cause is an old, half-forgotten, or merely ru-
mored crime, insult, or feud, the fugitive carries with him an air
of romantic mystery. Was he wrong or wronged? Can he return?
Does he sleep with one eye open? Here is the attraction of the
Genie in the bottle, the Wandering Jew, Ethan Brand, and the
countless wary lone riders of the cinema western.

11. Nobody knows where they came from and nobody knows where they went. They came in the
night and they left in the night. Some say that Uncle
Bud had to leave Tennessee when he came here because

53

he had been moonshining down there and had killed a man.

12. Uncle Bud was an educated man. He used to read the Bible quite a bit. He would get out in the shade of the house and read and chew a big cud of tobacco, the old homespun type. When he would get through chewing it, he would lay it up in the crack of the log cabin and let it dry out. Then he would use it for smoking tobacco later on when it dried out.

The remarks about arrival and departure have persisted because they convey a satisfying sense of mystery. They also reciprocate with the treasure motifs. This fondness for the Gothic touch is seen in the selection and retention of various remarks apparently intended to accentuate the peculiar or eccentric habits of the Long family. That they satisfy the urge to maintain or create a mystery is shown by the demonstrable conflict between the oral tradition and the available facts. The suggestion that Uncle Bud was educated ties in with the report of hidden finery related to earlier and better times. Property deeds in the county courthouse show that both Uncle Bud and Janey signed their names with an X, the mark of an illiterate. The suggestion of mystery about their destination is in conflict with another report that Uncle Bud sent at least one letter (probably dictated) back to his old neighbors in Kentucky, and that Frankie rode through the area on horseback several years after they had moved away.

SEX

Not the titillating sex of boy meets girl, the kind usually taken for granted in traditional narrative, but tabu sex and its offspring loom large in folk literature. The avoidance of incest is one of the oldest and strongest injunctions in the history of mankind, and is, therefore, a suitable topic for gossip and powerful drama.

13. There were Uncle Bud and Janey and Frankie. Janey was Uncle Bud's daughter. Nobody knows who Frankie's father was. They lived like a bunch of groundhogs up there. Just one room, and a little one at that, and no floor, and one bed was all they had for all of them.

14. One day two of the young fellows in the neighborhood were walking toward Bud Long's shack. Janey came running up to them, plopped herself down on her back on the ground, and stuck her foot up for one of them to see. Said he should take the thorn out of her foot. Whether she had a thorn or not, nobody knows, but the boy was a little bit embarrassed because she didn't have any clothes on under her dress.

Informants in this community are generally reticent about alluding to sex. Remarks about Frankie's unknown paternity turned up frequently. Presented guardedly and by indirection, the motif was clear—possible or even probable incest. People expressed concern about the family's sleeping accommodations and Janey's attraction for young men in the neighborhood.

One story told with considerable relish was about Uncle Bud's large supply of ax handles. A young man is reputed to have devised the scheme of making an ax handle for a gift for Uncle Bud as an excuse for the visit when he went to call on Janey. Since he called much oftener than Uncle Bud could wear out ax handles, a surplus accumulated.

NOVELTY & SHOCKERS

Ethnocentric bias leads to responses that range from amusement to shock when we are confronted by the unfamiliar. A middle-class housewife might swoon if she were to step into the killing room of a meat packing company, yet the workers there go about their duties in a welter of bawling and blood as routinely as other assembly-line employees tighten nuts and bolts. A businessman might feel a sense of panic in the embalming room of a busy mortuary, just as the embalmers might be uneasy if confronted by a complicated financial problem. There is a difference, however, for tales about events in the business world are uncommon, whereas tales about the dead are important fare, both in oral traditions and in formal literature. Motifs involving the unfamiliar, the mysterious, or the gruesome have their special kind of appeal, and they often combine with motifs of some of the other categories mentioned above.

> 15. When Mrs. Long died and the neighbors were there, Uncle Bud thought he should offer them something to eat. He went over to the bed where the corpse was laid out and rummaged around under the bed to find the meat box. He pulled out a part of a ham, squatted down and held it between his knees, and started slicing off meat for his guests. . . . The ladies didn't have any appetite.

This narrative, supplied by a number of informants with varying emphasis and detail, has survived because it is a vivid illustration of the deprived circumstances of the Long household. It tends to reinforce the numskull and fugitive motifs, and it parallels other shockers, such as dipping cooking water from the duckpond (see below), feeding the cow inside the shack, and sharing living quarters with chickens, goats, dogs, and pigs.

> 16. Janey came down the hill to see my grandmother. She had seven cents, and she wanted to borrow or buy a thimble. My grandmother asked her what had happened to her thimble, and Janey said she had lost it.

Said she had gone to the duckpond to get water to cook her beans, and she lost her thimble in the pond. They had a good spring up there behind the house, but Janey wouldn't bother to go up there for water.

17. Another thing about Uncle Bud, he used to buy corn. He had an old corncrib, and he seemed to think somebody would come and steal his corn. Nobody knew where their money came from, but he was always able to scrape up enough money to buy corn for cornbread. He used to take his corn, take it in the house, and throw it under the bed. Then he would nail board strips around the side and end of the bed to keep it from spilling out on the floor. Then he could pull it through the cracks and use it.

18. The Longs didn't have any table. When they used to eat, soup beans was about a three-times-a-day fare. Soup beans, cornbread, and either sorghum molasses or corn syrup. Uncle Bud used to take the bowl of beans, put it between his knees, and eat out of the bowl. When Janey or Frankie wanted some beans, they would hold their plate over, and he would give them beans. Same with the syrup or sorghum. He would put the pail between his knees, eat out of the pail, with the crumbs dropping in, and when Janey or Frankie wanted some, he would pour a bit and cut it off with his finger when he thought they had enough.

19. Frankie would carry his lunch to school in a syrup bucket. He always had the same thing. He had a container full of chunks of unworked butter and a piece of corn pone. The other children would come and peek to see what he had. He didn't seem to mind.

These narratives, some transcribed from tape recordings and some recalled from unrecorded conversations, illustrate the motifs that range from novelty to shock. The primitive table accommodations in the Long household immediately bring to mind similar deprivation as described in the widely popular fiddler and monologue piece, *The Arkansas Traveler*. It seems quite probable that *The Arkansas Traveler* served as a model for the rendition or the shaping of some of the Bud Long motifs.

FORMULA

Folklore generally, be it in the form of riddles, proverbs, tales, songs, or beliefs, is characterized by formulae. The magical charm of combinations of 3's or 7's, rhymes, stock epithets, and other easily recalled, frequently used devices appears to be the fundamental hallmark of oral traditions. The formula utterance is such a strong tradition that it may be used in self-contradictory contexts, such as the "false true-love" of ballad texts.

A. B. Chapman, repeating some observations about Uncle Bud after an interval of more than a year, remarked that Uncle Bud always used as many jennies to pull his wagon as the number of crossties in the load: a team of two for two ties, four jennies for four ties, six for six. Apparently six crossties on a wagon was his limit—or the limit allowable for narrative purposes among people familiar with teams and wagons. This formula turned up from time to time buried in various other contexts so that only reiteration called attention to it. Like the injection of a three, a seven, or a false true-love into a context which does not need it or does not even allow for it logically, this insistence on surplus jenny-power does not make sense. But the formula is established in folklore, which is enough reason for an experienced farmer to tell it with a straight face.

The fact is that a strong man can lift a crosstie to his shoulder and carry it alone, as the stevedores did in the old days when the tie barge pulled in to Clark's Landing. A team of jennies, even though they are smaller than dray horses, can pull a reasonable load uphill. And finally, the best evidence available about the team, the wagon, and the load is an old snapshot of Uncle Bud sitting on top of what appears to be a load of six crossties. He is driving two jennies. Interestingly, Mr. Chapman has seen the photograph, but his 2-4-6 utterance seems to take precedence over mere factual detail.

To check on this phenomenon further I seized the opportunity to show Earl Thomas a copy of the photograph just after he had remarked that Uncle Bud ordinarily hauled two ties, never more than three, behind two jennies. He studied the photograph for some time, handed it back to me and remarked, "Well, I guess you made a liar out of me. He's got six ties on the load—this time!"

Responses of informants vary considerably (as is true in any collection of folklore) according to the narrative skill of the individual. Beyond the matter of repertory, skill, and willingness, however, is an important element of attitude. As a rule, an informant approached with questions suggesting a search for factual information was unsatisfactory. Not one person interviewed, for example, could readily supply the year of the departure or Frankie's surname. Some of these same informants, approached a second time with banter about old gossip, brightened at once and offered an observation or a whole series of observations about Bud Long.

As the narratives moved from the matter-of-fact reports of Uncle Bud's contemporaries to the oral traditions of the younger generation, a process of selection winnowed out and emphasized the standard motifs. For the second- or third-generation narrator, precise name, time, and place become unimportant. It matters not whether the alleged events took place in this century or another. It was, in effect, "once upon a time." With the emphasis thus shifted from history to legend, the narrator who has no personal memory of his characters can perform the transformation of the apparently factual report that chickens roosted on Bud Long's bed by substituting the traveling anecdote of chickens on the meal barrel.

Informant A, one too young to have personal recollection, quoted a conversation supposed to be standard at the Longs' at bedtime:

"Janey, have you turned the chickens?"
"No, Paw."
"Well, turn them [to roost with tails pointing away from the bed] so they won't nasty the bed."

Informant B reported the same turning of the chickens, but in this instance the chickens were roosting on the meal barrel and were turned to keep them from spoiling the meal. Informant B is using a widely circulated anecdote about shiftless tenants who in other contexts also endure a leaky roof when it rains because they can't fix it in the rain, and who do not fix it in fair weather because it isn't leaking then—the numskull motif.

The Bud Long legend exists, not as a long, connected narrative, but in scattered anecdotal fragments as illustrated above. In other words, it exists as a truly traditional folk legend. If and when a skilled narrator weaves the motifs together and provides transitions and connectives, the Bud Long cycle as folk art will have had the kiss of death—conscious literary treatment.

The folk process of selection and re-creation has preserved and modified certain motifs. The end product of this folk process is a set of motifs that reflect what some investigators would call the "folk mind" or a "folk aesthetic." In other words, in the light of what is known about folk narrative, given the raw material in its setting and time for it to develop into an oral tradition, the development has followed an almost predictable pattern. Scattered anecdotes containing trickster, numskull, animal, fugitive, treasure, sex, and shocker motifs have persisted. Hundreds or even

60

thousands of other possible and even more factual observations of the Long family have fallen away.

From the limited point of view of the professional literary critic or literary historian—the professor of literature conditioned by refinements of aesthetic considerations of the great end-products of the literary process—the legend of the Long family is not literature. In fact, the professor of literature sees no legend in the sense of a connected narrative. To him, the material seems trivial, possibly childish, probably untrue, and certainly not worthy of his serious consideration.

But as one great folktale scholar has observed, to know the literary process fully, the scholar should avoid confining his attention to mere end-products. Great literature satisfies the intellectual and aesthetic needs of refined tastes; but great literature, like the visible portion of a floating iceberg, does not reveal at once the whole of which it is a part.[5]

To the folklorist, concerned with those aspects of the literary process analogous to the submerged portion of the literary iceberg, the Long narratives assume considerable significance. The fact that there is no neat, refined narrative at the folk level serves to authenticate the folk nature of the legend. As Richard Dorson has pointed out with considerable authority, the diffuse, fragmented nature of American folk legends is characteristic rather than anomalous.[6] Only after the journalists, the dramatists, or the promoters have discovered, refined, and displayed the materials do they begin to assume those characteristics that make them recognizable. Or, to put it another way, only when the unwritten literature becomes part of written literature does it ordinarily receive the label literature.

Oral beginnings, however, are a necessary part of the process —as they were in the background materials of Skipper Ireson, Ichabod Crane, Hiawatha, Ma Joad, Tristram, the Pardoner, Portia, or practically any other literary character or event one cares to mention. Examination of these folk materials reveals the less familiar workings of the literary process. Among other things, one learns that the selection, rejection, and adaptation process at the folk level puts emphasis on a range of motifs (such as those cited above) that is remarkably similar to the range of motifs which dominates belletristic literature.

The Legend as History

FORTUNATELY for the studies of folklore, literature, and history, serious investigation of the oral history of the folk at the grassroots level is becoming a growing concern of professional historians. A strong indication of this may be seen in the reception of Montell's *The Saga of Coe Ridge: A Study in Oral History*,[1] wherein the folklorist-historian has concerned himself with the grassroots history of a virtually unrecorded and undocumented community of people who were isolated, were generally unrespectable by the norms of their neighbors, and had the added disadvantage of being mostly black in a Southern setting.

In his preface (p. ix), Montell cites Homer C. Hockett, who has provided the rationale for many historians by stating that legends and traditions of the people should be avoided (by the historian) "for the simple reason that they cannot be traced to their origins." Montell's book demonstrates that traditions quite frequently can be traced to their origins, and that energetic field collection of oral traditions may yield a more reliable segment of history than can be obtained from scanty, falsified, or nonexistent documentary records.

This study of the Bud Long legend supports Montell's conclusions and extends them into a further consideration of oral literature. First, the oral traditions of the Clark's Landing area, judiciously analyzed, permit a reasonably consistent reconstruction of the otherwise virtually unrecorded life style of the principals. Second, winnowing out the dominant motifs of the cycle of anecdotes permits an examination of the intrusion of fiction into the legend-making phase of the folk memory. These two functions are not mutually contradictory.

If the legend of Bud Long is evaluated from the usual historical perspective, that is, along the lines of traditional academic historiography, it is not good history. The facts as recalled are too fragmentary. The information is sometimes self-contradictory. Except for a few faded, ill-identified photographs, there is virtually no documentation. A person like Bud Long, or Janey, or Frankie just does not get admitted to respectable historical research. Besides, none of them is associated with any event worthy of the historian's concern.

Amateur or commercial researchers who produce city, county, or state historical publications, and who do not necessarily subscribe to the prejudices of professional historians, frequently accept undocumented data, but their concern is not with Bud Long or his kind. They record for posterity, rather, the biographies of well-to-do landowners, successful local merchants, men of the medical and legal professions, sometimes teachers, and selected others who are important in local society—or who can pay the going price for a full-page portrait and some discreet autobiography. Since pride in family or community motivates publication of the ordinary local history, unimportant people are generally ignored in such publications, and the ragged segment of the society is positively censored out of the record.

Of course, Supreme Court decisions, treaties, and assassinations are more important than the questionable facts of the daily life of a citizen, just as the proprietor of a store or a lumber mill makes a more significant impression on a community than does any one of his virtually nameless customers or employees. It is right, then, that the historian be concerned with the record of the relatively more important events and people.

Bud Long and his family made an impression on a community, however. That impression may be more meaningful within the community than any number of well-documented reports of stirring events on a national or international level. A half-century later, Charlie Young can tell what Janey cooked for the wagon trip back to Tennessee, but he cannot recall the details of any Supreme Court decision during that same period. Earl Thomas can recall some details of Bud Long's harness for his legendary jennies from a similar distance in time, but he cannot give the details of any international treaty from that or any other distance in time. Combs Hicks recalls the time a rotten string broke and let Bud Long's pants fall down in Vertrees' store, but he fails to recall hundreds of other events from that era.

The point of these illustrations is that Bud and Janey and Frankie performed a subtle function in the Clark's Landing area. They were not important in the usual sense of importance—economic and social—but in an opposite way, as a kind of negative point of reference. Evidence in this study suggests that the folk develop their self-image, their aspirations and aversions, their sense of a set of social norms, by reference to models, not only in their contemporary scene but also in their folk history. Just as some people in the area of the Bud Long cycle aspired to be as well-to-do, as quick-witted, or as admired as Squire John Hardy Thomas, they avoided being as trashy as the outcasts of Whiskey Holler.

Depending on the orientation of the person being interviewed, and possibly conditioned by the context of the interview, responses to questions about the Long family ranged through hor-

65

ror, dismay, contempt, derision, and compassion. There was no indication that any member of the family could qualify for emulation in any way. This is precisely the source of the importance of the Longs in folk history, for they, more than many of their more "normal" contemporaries, helped to establish and maintain certain social norms. Theirs was the nadir rather than the zenith of a way of life.

Conclusion

THE systematic study of folklore involves collection of its many manifestations from the folk, followed by analysis of the collectanea. As in other disciplines, accuracy of observations or conclusions has a correlation with the number of representative samples studied.

The collection and analysis of American legends are needed to offset some of the misconceptions, both popular and academic, that have developed through misunderstandings, premature conclusions, and wishful thinking. Children's books which relate the quaint antics of Paul Bunyan and his blue ox, for instance, are much more likely to be identified as American folklore than are narratives about Bud Long or any of the hundreds of other American characters like him. This is true in spite of the fact that the Bunyan material is "fakelore," concocted by writers who have a mistaken impression of what American legends should be like.

Some academic intolerance of folk studies arises from honest

67

error. The presumably folk materials being rejected are actually fake materials. The nonspecialist's conception of folklore is ordinarily conditioned by whatever bears the label and is most readily available. Since it is the "fakelore" of the marketplace that clamors for attention, it is the "fakelore" of the marketplace that is quite rightly regarded with scorn.

Two memorable and significant coinages in folklore studies are the word folklore by William Thoms, a nineteenth-century scholar, and the word fakelore by Richard Dorson, who, well over a century after Thoms's coinage, first sounded the alarm about the appropriation of folklore by the money-writers. A portion of Dorson's chapter on folk heroes in *American Folklore*[1] deserves quotation:

> Paul Bunyan and his fellows rest on little or no oral tradition and on no historical prototypes. The spirit of gargantuan whimsy oozing through the contemporary heroes reflects no actual mood of lumberjacks, cowboys, or steelworkers but only the childlike fancies of money-writers. Indeed the chief folklore connected with them lies in the mistaken idea that they are folk heroes—an idea widely held by school-teachers, librarians, and the public and assiduously fostered by writers and promoters. The names and antics of these occupational giants have now elbowed aside the Greek and Roman gods and myths who once dominated the minds of American children.

As I indicated earlier in this study, the typical American folk legend, though devoid of the unity one finds in a written composition, is nevertheless a functioning unit of unwritten literature. It has its own aesthetic qualities in its cultural setting, and it performs certain social functions related to spiritual, moral, or social values, in addition to its "reaffirmation of social cohesion."[2]

The study of the folk legend is primarily the study of literature, for the folk legend is a form of literature, and, like more advanced forms of literature which are written rather than told, may be subjected to philosophical, historical, and other kinds of analysis. The legend of Bud Long is a particularly good example for display because it so precisely illustrates the casual, fragmented nature of such material in its cultural setting. This cluster of unadorned narratives illustrates the folk process—selective change in oral tradition. Through all the complicated process of forgetting, remembering, and reconstructing, the folk narrators have done away with much that was particular and have substituted more commonplace elements. In addition to this leveling process, the folk have been selective enough to demonstrate the grassroots interests that are reflected in the motifs of folklore elsewhere and in much of the popular literature of both European and American tradition.

It is this underpinning of the literary traditions that should be of special interest to the literary historian and literary critic. Collections and studies of oral literature may eventually give added support to the impressions suggested here—that art literature is a complex rendition of selected motifs of popular literature, that popular literature is a complex rendition of selected motifs of folk literature, and that all these are varied aspects of the verbal expressions of mankind. To study the phenomenon of literature, one must examine the whole range of expression, from its deceptively simple oral sources to the full orchestration of these and their intermediate blendings as they are used by the great artist of belletristic culture. This broad-spectrum study may be developed only by increasing the emphasis on folk literature, heretofore the most neglected aspect of literary investigation.

Of the various genres of folk literature, the legend in particular has recently come under intensive scrutiny by folklorists, who are raising fundamental questions about its definition, scope, and role. *American Folk Legend*[3] is a collection of papers read at a symposium on legend at the University of California at Los Angeles. The fourteen papers by well-known folklorists published in the volume reveal that folklorists are not entirely in agreement about what they want to call legend, how to collect and study legend, and how to distinguish folk legend from popular, literary, or promotional legend. They do agree, however, that systematic examination of American legendry has hardly begun.

Exposure of legendary material in a community may be accomplished in many different ways. The choice in this instance has been to combine scientific interest and method with the humanistic notion that Uncle Bud's place in oral history is worthy of study, that a poet might do Janey as much justice as a social scientist could, and that the general reader has as much need as the scholar to ponder our American heritage.

An Afterword

CHANGES in the landscape and community accelerate with the passage of time. During the few months that have elapsed since the first lines of this study were set down, the State of Kentucky has approved a highway project, surveyed and acquired the right-of-way, and constructed a four-lane toll road between Owensboro and Bowling Green.

The directions for reaching Clark's Landing are different now because a deep fill blocks Clifty Hollow Road. The traveler, then, must take a longer way around via a gravel road that runs parallel to the new turnpike. Broad twin bands of asphalt paving wind over the ridge where Uncle Bud lived and worked. Cars and trucks whiz through the terrain which once provided forage for Bud Long's free-ranging jennies. The vacant Indian caves tremble at the passing of each roaring truck.

Upstream, at the juncture of the Gasper and Barren rivers, Dr. L. Y. Lancaster, present owner of the Sally's Rock promontory, complains that thieves have discovered and dug up his secret patch of ginseng. He had been proud of his ownership, for he had learned that Sally Beck herself had once tended a patch there. He believes it unlikely that the ginseng will be restored. It is slow developing and easily destroyed.

Even the everlasting spring that once fed Uncle Bud's duck pond and formed the headwater of a tributary of Maxey Creek appears to be failing. The clearing of the land and the construction of a highway do not help the water storage capability of a small upland area.

Part of the old Cardwell farm that adjoined Bud Long's land recently brought approximately one hundred times as much per acre as Uncle Bud had to pay. The land is unfit for growing corn, but the townsman who bought it has a different use in mind: a site for a week-end cottage.

The fragile local legend has changed, also. One can still get a response from the loafers around the stove in Givens's store, but it is not the unselfconscious response of earlier times. The local people began to take a deliberate stance when responding to questions after a young woman in the store suddenly asked me, "Are you going to write a book about Uncle Bud?"

Walton Deweese, too young to know the principals directly, but recalling his father's anecdotes, made a point of bringing his elderly father to my home on a Sunday afternoon. Walton's father is retired, a resident of Florida, and he was visiting his Kentucky family. He told about the jennies and the chickens on the meal barrel. He regretted that he could recall nothing about Mrs. Long. But he did tell a new tale about Uncle Bud. However, the circumstances of the collection of this and other late-arriving narratives are different from the earlier circumstances. It is one thing to collect unobtrusively; it is another thing to be solicited to accept information. When informants have become conscious of their role in reporting a legend, or when they begin to think of their material as legendary, their information becomes less useful if the object has been to investigate the undisturbed beginnings of a legend-making process.

The folk legend of Uncle Bud Long, like Dr. Lancaster's ginseng patch, has been dug up. Whatever is left is just a reminder of what once flourished in natural seclusion.

Notes

INTRODUCTION

1. (Bloomington: Indiana University Press, 1954). Price's objective was to sort out the historically valid information, whereas the objective in this study is to document legend-making at its source.

THE NARRATIVES AS FOLK LITERATURE

1. Ph.D. dissertation, Indiana University, 1949. Jansen's purpose, as stated in his introduction (p. ii), was "to compare fact and folklore: to present a folk hero as a folk hero and as an historical figure."

2. See note 1 to Introduction, above.

3. Richard Dorson, ed., *Davy Crockett, American Comic Legend* (New York, 1939).

4. By Stith Thompson (Bloomington: Indiana University Press, 1955-1957).

5. Stith Thompson, "Story-Writers and Story-Tellers," in *Philologica: The Malone Anniversary Studies*, edited by Thomas A. Kirby and Henry Bosley Woolf (Baltimore: Johns Hopkins Press, 1949). In his article, Dr. Thompson reflects a degree of impatience with the blindness in a certain kind of academic intolerance which leads to professed rejection of folk studies by scholars devoted to the "standard" authors, periods, and genres.

6. Richard Dorson, "Defining American Folk Legend," in *American Folklore and the Historian* (Chicago: University of Chicago Press, 1971).

THE LEGEND AS HISTORY

1. William Lynwood Montell (Knoxville: University of Tennessee Press, 1970).

CONCLUSION

1. (Chicago: University of Chicago Press, 1959), pp. 214-15.

2. Folklorists are indebted in S. I. Hayakawa for this very appropriate phrase. It occurs in his popular book on semantics, *Language in Thought and Action* (New York: Harcourt, Brace, 1949). Hayakawa used the phrase in describing the function of "ritual utterances," with no particular indication that such utterances were folkloristic. Properly considered, however, all verbal folklore is in some way a "reaffirmation of social cohesion."

3. Edited by Wayland D. Hand (Berkeley: University of California Press 1971).

75

Informants

The principal sources for this study are field-collected oral traditions. Although many other informants supplied valuable information and insights, the few listed below made significant contributions. I am indebted to them all.

MR. CLARENCE BELCHER, Morgantown Road, who was another tie-hacker in his prime.

MRS. THOMAS BELCHER, Bowling Green, who was a Hayes, who filled in details others forgot.

MR. B. V. CARDWELL, Morgantown Road, who recalls the time the hen laid an egg on the bed, and whose grandchildren love his Bud Long tales better than any other kind.

MR. ARTHUR BLAINE CHAPMAN, Guy Road, who recalls the hard work of tie-hacking with little pleasure.

MRS. ARTHUR BLAINE CHAPMAN, who was a Cardwell and who helpfully dug up some old photographs.

MR. LEON CHAPMAN, Clark's Landing Road, too young to know the principals but an inheritor of the legend.

MR. BOB CLARK, Indianapolis, son of Elvis, too young to know the principals but an inheritor of the legend.

MR. ELVIS CLARK, Chicago, once a resident and neighbor.

MRS. EUTHA CLARK, Clark's Landing, who was a Meador and an inheritor of the legend.

MR. HAROLD CLARK, Clark's Landing, who watched the steamers come and go, and who dug up some old photographs.

MR. DEWEY DEWEESE, of Florida, who dropped in during his vacation to tell more about Uncle Bud.

MR. JESSE HENDERSON, Sugar Grove Road, born in 1887, the oldest informant.

MR. A. C. HICKS, Morgantown Road, who thought he could remember when the Longs arrived in Warren County.

MRS. HETTIE NEWTON HOWARD, Morgantown Road, who thought Janey was Uncle Bud's wife.

MRS. ANDY HUGHES, Highland Road, who was a Clark and who recalls Janey's baskets.

MR. WILLIS JUSTICE, Highland Road, who traded with Uncle Bud.

MRS. JOHN McDANIELS, Bowling Green, present owner of Bud Long Hill, who provided information from her files.

MR. ANDREW MANNING, Death Valley Road, who lived and worked nearby.

MR. EARL MANNING, Death Valley Road, Andrew's son, too young to know the principals but an inheritor of the legend, which he narrates with verve.

MRS. E. E. SHARER, Bowling Green, who was a Hayes and who recalls the miller's toll that was thrown to the chickens.

MR. EARL THOMAS, Guy Road, who can describe Uncle Bud's team harness and wagon.

MR. WILL THOMAS, Bowling Green, who taught in the one-room school.

MR. FEALON WHITE, Morgantown Road, who can recall the words and tune of Frankie's song.

MR. C. W. YOUNG, Death Valley Road, a retired river pilot and farmer who lived nearby.

MRS. MAE YOUNG, Death Valley Road, who felt compassion for Janey.

*This book has been set in
Monotype Bembo, a typeface
modeled after a roman cut
by Francesco Griffo for
the Venetian printer
Aldus Manutius in the
late 15 th century.*

*Composition & printing
by Heritage Printers, Inc.*

*Binding by Carolina Ruling
and Binding Co., Inc.*

Design by Jonathan Greene